Treasures from the Spiritual Classics

REVELATIONS OF DIVINE LOVE
by
JULIAN OF NORWICH

Compiled by
Roger L. Roberts

Morehouse-Barlow Co., Inc.
Wilton, Connecticut

First USA edition published 1982
Morehouse-Barlow Co., Inc.
78 Danbury Road
Wilton, Connecticut 06897

Printed in the United States of America

PREFACE

'This is a Revelation of Love that Jesus Christ, our endless bliss, made in Sixteen Shewings, or Revelations particular.'

Such, in the author's own opening words, is the concise description of the outstanding work of English mediaeval mysticism from which the extracts which follow are taken. The author's name was Julian. She was born in 1342 and lived until at least 1413. She was probably a Benedictine nun and for most of her long life was certainly an anchoress at Norwich. As an anchoress she lived a solitary life of prayer and silence and self-discipline, withdrawn from the world, in a small room (or 'cell') attached to an ancient parish church in the city, where over the years pilgrims and penitents would resort to her to seek spiritual counsel.

Julian was, by her own account, a little over thirty years old and at death's door with a grave illness when she experienced, within the space of a few hours, a series of ecstatic visions, or "shewings", of the love of the Blessed Trinity and, most vividly, of the Passion of Christ Crucified. The overwhelming impact of this paranormal experience was such as to govern the rest of her days. She made a sudden recovery from her sickness and spent the next twenty years in constant meditation on the meaning of what had befallen her. The final fruit of that prolonged meditation is her famous book.

Despite the gulf of years separating the book's first appearance in 1393 from modern times, and despite the inevitably antique vocabulary employed by the author, it has a timeless quality of extraordinary power and is also a notably human document. Julian's capacity for heightened emotion is matched by her gift for sober and exact observation, by saving humour, and by true humility; she never presumes to place herself above her 'even-Christians' (her delightful term for fellow-believers) and is careful always to accept the unquestioned authority of the Church in matters of faith. But her mystical insight is all her own, as she finds the solution to all the problems of sin and suffering in the invincible reality of the Love of God. Her book is one of the most moving testimonies ever written to that Love's eternal glory and power.

R.L.R.

The extracts which follow are reprinted from Julian of Norwich's *Revelations of Divine Love* edited by Grace Warrack from the MS in the British Museum, and published (tenth edition) in 1934 by Methuen & Co Ltd.

THE REVELATION

THESE Revelations were shewed to a simple creature unlettered, the year of our Lord 1373, the Eighth day of May. Which creature [had] afore desired three gifts of God. The First was mind of His Passion; the Second was bodily sickness in youth, at thirty years of age; the Third was to have of God's gift three wounds.

As to the First, methought I had some feeling in the Passion of Christ, but yet I desired more by the grace of God. Methought I would have been that time with Mary Magdalene, and with other that were Christ's lovers, and therefore I desired a bodily sight wherein I might have more knowledge of the bodily pains of our Saviour and of the compassion of our Lady and of all His true lovers that saw, that time, His pains. For I would be one of them and suffer with Him. Other sight nor shewing of God desired I never none, till the soul were disparted from the body. The cause of this petition was that after the shewing I should have the more true mind in the Passion of Christ.

The Second came to my mind with contrition; [I] freely desiring that sickness [to be] so hard as to death, that I might in that sickness receive all my rites of Holy Church, myself thinking that I should die, and that all creatures might suppose the same that saw me: for I would have no manner of comfort of earthly life. In this sickness I desired to have all manner of pains bodily and ghostly that I should have if I should die, (with all the dreads and tempests of the fiends) except the out-passing of the soul. And this I meant for [that] I would be purged, by the mercy of God, and afterward live more to the worship of God because of that sickness. And that for the more furthering in my death: for I desired to be soon with my God.

These two desires of the Passion and the sickness I desired with a condition, saying thus: *Lord, Thou knowest what I would,—if it be Thy will that I have it—; and if it be not Thy will, good Lord, be not displeased: for I will nought but as Thou wilt.*

For the Third [petition], by the grace of God and teaching of Holy Church I conceived a mighty desire to receive three wounds in my life: that is to say, the wound of very contrition, the wound of kind compassion, and the wound of steadfast longing toward God. And all this last petition I asked without any condition.

These two desires aforesaid passed from my mind, but the third dwelled with me continually.

And when I was thirty years old and a half, God sent me a bodily sickness, in which I lay three days and three nights; and on the fourth night I took all my rites of Holy Church, and weened not to have lived till day. And after this I languored forth two days and two nights, and on the third night I weened often-times to have passed; and so weened they that were with me.

And being in youth as yet, I thought it great sorrow to die;—but for nothing that was in earth that meliked to live for, nor for no pain that I had fear of: for I trusted in God of His mercy. But it was to have lived that I might have loved God better, and longer time, that I might have the more knowing and loving of God in bliss of Heaven. For methought all the time that I had lived here so little and so short in regard of that endless bliss,—I thought [it was as] nothing. Wherefore I thought: *Good Lord, may my living no longer be to Thy worship!* And I understood by my reason and by my feeling of my pains that I should die; and I assented fully with all the will of my heart to be at God's will.

Thus I dured till day, and by then my body was dead from the middle downwards, as to my feeling. Then was I minded to be set upright, backward leaning, with help,—for to have more freedom of my heart to be at God's will, and thinking on God while my life would last.

My Curate was sent for to be at my ending, and by that time when he came I had set my eyes, and might not speak. He set the Cross before my face and said: *I have brought thee the Image of thy Maker and Saviour: look thereupon and comfort thee therewith.*

Methought I was well [as it was], for my eyes were set uprightward unto Heaven, where I trusted to come by the mercy of God; but nevertheless I assented to set my eyes on the face of the Crucifix, if I might; and so I did. For methought I might longer dure to look evenforth than right up.

After this my sight began to fail, and it was all dark about me in the chamber, as if it had been night, save in the Image of the Cross whereon I beheld a common light; and I wist not how. All that was away from the Cross was of horror to me, as if it had been greatly occupied by the fiends.

After this the upper part of my body began to die, so far forth that scarcely I had any feeling;—with shortness of breath. And then

11

I weened in sooth to have passed.

And in this [moment] suddenly all my pain was taken from me, and I was as whole (and specially in the upper part of my body) as ever I was afore.

I marvelled at this sudden change; for methought it was a privy working of God, and not of nature. And yet by the feeling of this ease I trusted never the more to live; nor was the feeling of this ease any full ease unto me: for methought I had liefer have been delivered from this world.

Then came suddenly to my mind that I should desire the second wound of our Lord's gracious gift: that my body might be fulfilled with mind and feeling of His blessed Passion. For I would that His pains were my pains, with compassion and afterward longing to God. But in this I desired never bodily sight nor shewing of God, but compassion such as a kind soul might have with our Lord Jesus, that for love would be a mortal man: and therefore I desired to suffer with Him.

12

In this [moment] suddenly I saw the red blood trickle down from under the Garland hot and freshly and right plenteously, as it were in the time of His Passion when the Garland of thorns was pressed on His blessed head who was both God and Man, the same that suffered thus for me. I conceived truly and mightily that it was Himself shewed it me, without any mean.

And in the same Shewing suddenly the Trinity fulfilled my heart most of joy. And so I understood it shall be in heaven without end to all that shall come there. For the Trinity is God: God is the Trinity; the Trinity is our Maker and Keeper, the Trinity is our everlasting love and everlasting joy and bliss, by our Lord Jesus Christ. And this was shewed in the First [Shewing] and in all: for where Jesus appeareth, the blessed Trinity is understood, as to my sight.

THE GOODNESS OF GOD

In this same time our Lord shewed me a spiritual sight of His homely loving.

I saw that He is to us everything that is good and comfortable for us: He is our clothing that for love wrappeth us, claspeth us, and all encloseth us for tender love, that He may never leave us; being to us all-thing that is good, as to mine understanding.

Also in this He shewed me a little thing, the quantity of an hazel-nut, in the palm of my hand; and it was as round as a ball. I looked thereupon with eye of my understanding, and thought: *What may this be?* And it was answered generally thus: *It is all that is made.* I marvelled how it might last, for methought it might suddenly have fallen to naught for little[ness]. And I was answered in my understanding: *It lasteth, and ever shall [last] for that God loveth it.* And so All-thing hath the Being by the love of God.

In this Little Thing I saw three properties.

14

The first is that God made it, the second is that God loveth it, the third, that God keepeth it. But what is to me verily the Maker, the Keeper, and the Lover,—I cannot tell; for till I am Substantially oned to Him, I may never have full rest nor very bliss: that is to say, till I be so fastened to Him, that there is right nought that is made betwixt my God and me.

It needeth us to have knowing of the littleness of creatures and to hold as nought allthing that is made, for to love and have God that is unmade. For this is the cause why we be not all in ease of heart and soul: that we seek here rest in those things that are so little, wherein is no rest, and know not our God that is All-mighty, All-wise, All-good. For He is the Very Rest. God willeth to be known, and it pleaseth Him that we rest in Him; for all that is beneath Him sufficeth not us. And this is the cause why that no soul is rested till it is made nought as to all things that are made. When it is willingly made nought, for love, to have Him that is all, then is it able to receive spiritual rest.

Also our Lord God shewed that it is full great pleasance to Him that a helpless soul come to Him simply and plainly and homely. For this is the natural yearnings of the soul, by the touching of the Holy Ghost (as by the understanding that I have in this Shewing): *God, of Thy Goodness, give me Thyself: for Thou art enough to me, and I may nothing ask that is less that may be full worship to Thee; and if I ask anything that is less, ever me wanteth,—but only in Thee I have all.*

And these words are full lovely to the soul, and full near touch they the will of God and His Goodness. For His Goodness comprehendeth all His creatures and all His blessed works, and overpasseth without end. For He is the endlessness, and He hath made us only to Himself, and restored us by His blessed Passion, and keepeth us in His blessed love; and all this of His Goodness.

This Shewing was made to learn our soul wisely to cleave to the Goodness of God.

And in that time the custom of our praying was brought to mind: how we use for lack of understanding and knowing of Love, to take many means [whereby to beseech Him].

Then saw I truly that it is more worship to God, and more very delight, that we faithfully pray to Himself of His Goodness and cleave thereunto by His Grace, with true understanding, and steadfast by love, than if we took all the means that heart can think. For if we took all these means, it is too little, and not full worship to God: but in His Goodness is all the whole, and *there* faileth right nought.

For this, as I shall tell, came to my mind in the same time: We pray to God for [the sake of] His holy flesh and His precious blood, His holy Passion, His dearworthy death and wounds: and all the blessed kindness, the endless life that we have of all this, is His Goodness. And we pray Him for [the sake of] His sweet Mother's love that Him bare; and all the help we have of her is of His Goodness. And we pray by His holy Cross that he died on, and all the virtue and the help that we have of the Cross, it is of His Goodness. And on the same wise, all the help that we have of special saints and all the blessed Company of Heaven, the dearworthy love and endless friendship that we have of them, it is of His Goodness. For God of His Goodness hath ordained means to help us, full fair and many: of which the chief and principal mean is the blessed nature that He took of the Maid, with all the means that go afore and come after which belong to our redemption and to endless salvation. Wherefore it pleaseth Him that we seek Him and worship through means, understanding that He is the Goodness of all.

For the Goodness of God is the highest prayer, and it cometh down to the lowest part of our need. It quickeneth our soul and bringeth it on life, and maketh it for to waxen in grace and virtue. It is nearest in nature; and readiest in grace: for *it* is the same grace that the soul seeketh, and ever shall seek till we

18

know verily that He hath us all in Himself enclosed.

For He hath no despite of that He hath made, nor hath He any disdain to serve us at the simplest office that to our body belongeth in nature, for love of the soul that He hath made to His own likeness.

For as the body is clad in the cloth, and the flesh in the skin, and the bones in the flesh, and the heart in the whole, so are we, soul and body, clad in the Goodness of God and enclosed. Yea, and more homely: for all these may waste and wear away, but the Goodness of God is ever whole; and more near to us, without any likeness; for truly our Lover desireth that our soul cleave to Him with all its might, and that we be evermore cleaving to His Goodness. For of all things that heart may think, this pleaseth most God, and soonest speedeth [the soul].

'ALL IS WELL DONE'

And after this I saw God in a Point, that is to say, in mine understanding,—by which sight I saw that He is in all things.

I beheld and considered, seeing and knowing in sight, with a soft dread, and thought: *What is sin?*

For I saw truly that God doeth all-thing, be it never so little. And I saw truly that nothing is done by hap nor by adventure, but all things by the foreseeing wisdom of God: if it be hap or adventure in the sight of man, our blindness and our unforesight is the cause. For the things that are in the foreseeing wisdom of God from without beginning, (which rightfully and worshipfully and continually He leadeth to the best end,) as they come about fall to us suddenly, ourselves unwitting; and thus by our blindness and our unforesight we say: these be haps and adventures. But to our Lord God they be not so.

Wherefore me behoveth needs to grant that

all-thing that is done, it is well-done: for our Lord God doeth all. For in this time the working of creatures was not shewed, but [the working] of our Lord God in the creature: for He is in the Mid-point of all thing, and all He doeth. And I was certain He doeth no sin.

And here I saw verily that sin is no deed: for in all this was not sin shewed. And I would no longer marvel in this, but beheld our Lord, what He would shew.

And thus, as much as it might be for the time, the rightfulness of God's working was shewed to the soul.

Rightfulness hath two fair properties: it is right and it is full. And so are all the works of our Lord God: thereto needeth neither the working of mercy nor grace: for they be all rightful: wherein faileth nought.

But in another time He gave a Shewing for the beholding of sin nakedly, as I shall tell: where He useth working of mercy and grace.

And this vision was shewed, to mine understanding, for that our Lord would have the soul turned truly unto the beholding of Him, and generally of all His works. For they are full good; and all His doings are easy and sweet, and to great ease bringing the soul that is turned from the beholding of the blind Deeming of man unto the fair sweet Deeming of our Lord God. For a man beholdeth some deeds well done and some deeds evil, but our Lord beholdeth them not so: for as all that hath being in nature is of Godly making, so is all that is done, in property of God's doing. For it is easy to understand that the best deed is well done: and so well as the best deed is done—the highest—so well is the least deed done; and all thing in its property and in the order that our Lord hath ordained it to from without beginning. For there is no doer but He.

I saw full surely that he changeth never His purpose in no manner of thing, nor never shall, without end. For there was no thing unknown to Him in His rightful ordinance from without beginning. And therefore all-thing was set in order ere anything was made, as it should stand without end; and no manner of thing shall fail of that point. For He made all things in fulness of goodness, and therefore the blessed Trinity is ever full pleased in all His works.

And all this shewed He full blissfully, signifying thus: *See! I am God: see! I am in all thing: see! I do all thing: see! I lift never mine hands off my works, nor ever shall, without end: see! I lead all thing to the end I ordained it to from without beginning, by the same Might, Wisdom and Love whereby I made it. How should any thing be amiss?*

Thus mightily, wisely, and lovingly was the soul examined in this Vision. Then saw I soothly that me behoved, of need, to assent, with great reverence enjoying in God.

THE PASSION OF CHRIST

Then said our good Lord Jesus Christ: *Art thou well pleased that I suffered for thee?* I said: *Yea, good Lord, I thank Thee; Yea, good Lord, blessed mayst Thou be.* Then said Jesus, our kind Lord: *If thou art pleased, I am pleased: it is a joy, a bliss, an endless satisfying to me that ever suffered I Passion for thee; and if I might suffer more, I would suffer more.*

In this feeling my understanding was lifted up into Heaven, and there I saw three heavens: of which sight I marvelled greatly. And though I see three heavens—and all in the blessed manhood of Christ—none is more, none is less, none is higher, none is lower, but [they are] even-like in bliss.

For the First Heaven, Christ shewed me His Father; in no bodily likeness, but in His property and in His working. That is to say, I saw in Christ that the Father is. The working of the Father is this, that He giveth meed to

His Son Jesus Christ. This gift and this meed is so blissful to Jesus that His Father might have given Him no meed that might have pleased Him better. The first heaven, that is the pleasing of the Father, shewed to me as one heaven; and it was full blissful: for He is full pleased with all the deeds that Jesus hath done about our salvation. Wherefore we be not only His by His buying, but also by the courteous gift of His Father we be His bliss, we be His meed, we be His worship, we be His crown. (And this was a singular marvel and a full delectable beholding, that we be His crown!) This that I say is so great bliss to Jesus that He setteth at nought all His travail, and His hard Passion, and His cruel and shameful death.

And in these words: *If that I might suffer more, I would suffer more*,—I saw in truth that as often as He *might* die, so often He *would*, and love should never let Him have rest till He had done it. And I beheld with great diligence for to learn how often He would die if He might. And verily the number passed mine understanding and my wits so far that my reason might not, nor could, comprehend it. And when He had thus oft died, or should, yet He would set it at nought, for love: for all seemeth Him but little in regard of His love.

For though the sweet manhood of Christ might suffer but once, the goodness in Him may never cease of proffer: every day He is ready to the same, if it might be. For if He said He would for my love make new Heavens and new Earth, it were but little in comparison; for this might be done every day if He would, without any travail. But to die for my love so often that the number passeth creature's reason, it is the highest proffer that our Lord God might make to man's soul, as to my sight. Then meaneth He thus: *How should it not be that I should not do for thy love all that I might of deeds which grieve me not, sith I would, for thy love, die so often, having no regard to my hard pains?*

And here saw I, for the Second Beholding in this blessed Passion *the love that made Him to suffer passeth as far all His pains as Heaven is above Earth.* For the pains was a noble, worshipful deed done in a time by the working of love: but Love was without beginning, is, and shall be without ending. For which love He said full sweetly these words: *If I might suffer more, I would suffer more.* He said not, *If it were needful to suffer more*: for though it were not needful, if He *might* suffer more, He would.

This deed, and this work about our salvation, was ordained as well as God might ordain it. And here I saw a Full Bliss in Christ: for His bliss should not have been full, if it might any better have been done.

And in these three words: *It is a joy, a bliss, an endless satisfying to me*, were shewed three heavens, as thus: For the joy, I understood the pleasure of the Father; and for the bliss, the worship of the Son; and for the endless satisfying, the Holy Ghost. The Father is

27

pleased, the Son is worshipped, the Holy Ghost is satisfied.

And here saw I, for the Third Beholding in His blissful Passion: that is to say, *the Joy and the Bliss that make Him to be well-satisfied in it.* For our Courteous Lord shewed His Passion to me in five manners: of which the first is the bleeding of the head; the second is, discolouring of His face; the third is, the plenteous bleeding of the body, in seeming [as] from the scourging; the fourth is, the deep dying:—these four are aforetold for the pains of the Passion. And the fifth is [this] that was shewed for the joy and the bliss of the Passion.

For it is God's will that we have true enjoying with Him in our salvation, and therein He willeth [that] we be mightily comforted and strengthened; and thus willeth He that merrily with His grace our soul be occupied. For we are His bliss: for in us He enjoyeth without end; and so shall we in Him, with His grace.

And all that He hath done for us, and doeth, and ever shall, was never cost nor charge to Him, nor might be, but only that [which] He did in our manhood, beginning at the sweet Incarnation and lasting to the Blessed Uprise on Easter-morrow: so long dured the cost and the charge about our redemption in *deed*: of [the] which deed He enjoyeth endlessly, as it is aforesaid.

Jesus willeth that we take heed to the bliss that is in the blessed Trinity [because] of our salvation and that *we* desire to have as much spiritual enjoying, with His grace, (as it is aforesaid): that is to say, that the enjoying of our salvation be [as] like to the joy that Christ hath of our salvation as it may be while we are here.

All the Trinity wrought in the Passion of Christ, ministering abundance of virtues and plenty of grace to us by Him: but only the Maiden's Son suffered: whereof all the blessed Trinity endlessly enjoyeth. All this was shewed in these words: *Art thou well pleased?*—and by that other word that Christ said: *If thou art pleased, then am I pleased;*—as if He said: *It is joy and satisfying enough to me, and I ask nought else of thee for my travail but that I might well please thee.*

And in this He brought to mind the property of a glad giver. A glad giver taketh but little heed of the thing that he giveth, but all his desire and all his intent is to please him and solace him to whom he giveth it. And if the receiver take the gift highly and thankfully, then the courteous giver setteth at nought all his cost and all his travail, for joy and delight that he hath pleased and solaced him that he loveth. Plenteously and fully was this shewed.

Think also wisely of the greatness of this word '*ever*'. For in it was shewed an high knowing of love that *He* hath in our salvation, with manifold joys that follow of the Passion of Christ. One is that He rejoiceth that He hath done it in deed, and He shall no more suffer; another, that He bought us from endless pains of hell.

LOVE CONQUERS SIN

And after this our Lord shewed Himself more glorified, as to my sight, than I saw Him before [in the Shewing] wherein I was learned that our soul shall never have rest till it cometh to Him, knowing that He is fulness of joy, homely and courteous, blissful and very life.

Our Lord Jesus oftentimes said: *I it am, I it am: I it am that is highest, I it am that thou lovest, I it am that thou enjoyest, I it am that thou servest, I it am that thou longest for, I it am that thou desirest, I it am that thou meanest, I it am that is all. I it am that Holy Church preacheth and teacheth thee, I it am that shewed me here to thee.* The number of the words passeth my wit and all my understanding and all my powers. And they are the highest, as to my sight: for therein is comprehended—I cannot tell,—but the joy that

I saw in the Shewing of them passeth all that heart may wish for and soul may desire. Therefore the words be not declared here; but every man after the grace that God giveth him in understanding and loving, receive them in our Lord's meaning.

After this the Lord brought to my mind the longing that I had to Him afore. And I saw that nothing letted me but sin. And so I looked, generally, upon us all, and me-thought: *If sin had not been, we should all have been clean and like to our Lord, as He made us.*

And thus, in my folly, afore this time often I wondered why by the great foreseeing wisdom of God the beginning of sin was not letted: for then, methought, all should have been well. This stirring [of mind] was much to be forsaken, but nevertheless mourning and sorrow I made therefor, without reason and discretion.

But Jesus, who in this Vision informed me of all that is needful to me, answered by this word and said: *It behoved that there should be sin; but all shall be well, and all shall be well, and all manner of thing shall be well.*

In this naked word *sin*, our Lord brought to my mind, generally, *all that is not good*, and the shameful despite and the utter noughting that He bare for us in this life, and His dying; and all the pains and passions of all His creatures, ghostly and bodily; (for we be all partly noughted, and we shall be noughted following our Master, Jesus, till we be full purged, that is to say, till we be fully noughted of our deadly flesh and of all our inward affections which are not very good;) and the beholding of this, with all pains that ever were or ever shall be,—and with all these I understand the Passion of Christ for most pain, and overpassing. All this was shewed in a touch and quickly passed over into comfort: for our good Lord would not that the soul were affeared of this terrible sight.

But I saw not *sin*: for I believe it hath no manner of substance nor no part of being, nor could it be known but by the pain it is cause of.

And thus pain, *it* is something, as to my sight, for a time; for it purgeth, and maketh us to know ourselves and to ask mercy. For the Passion of our Lord is comfort to us against all this, and so is His blessed will. And for the tender love that our good Lord hath to all that shall be saved, He comforteth readily and sweetly, signifying thus: *It is sooth that sin is cause of all this pain; but all shall be well, and all shall be well, and all manner [of] thing shall be well.*

These words were said full tenderly, showing no manner of blame to me nor to any that shall be saved. Then were it a great unkindness to blame or wonder on God for my sin, since He blameth not me for sin.

And in these words I saw a marvellous high mystery hid in God, which mystery He shall openly make known to us in Heaven: in which knowing we shall verily see the cause why He suffered sin to come. In which sight we shall endlessly joy in our Lord God.

Thus I saw how Christ hath compassion on us for the cause of sin. And right as I was afore in the [shewing of the] Passion of Christ fulfilled with pain and compassion, like so in this [sight] I was fulfilled, in part, with compassion of all mine even-Christians—for that well, well beloved people that shall be saved. For God's servants, Holy Church, shall be shaken in sorrow and anguish, tribulation in this world, as men shake a cloth in the wind.

And as to this our Lord answered in this manner: *A great thing shall I make hereof in Heaven of endless worship and everlasting joys.*

Yea, so far forth I saw, that our Lord joyeth of the tribulations of His servants, with ruth and compassion. On each person that He loveth, to His bliss for to bring [them], He layeth something that is no blame in His sight, whereby they are blamed and despised in this world, scorned, mocked, and outcasted. And this He doeth for to hinder the harm that they should take from the pomp and the vain-glory of this wretched life, and make their way ready to come to Heaven, and up-raise them in His bliss everlasting. For He saith: *I shall wholly break you of your vain affections and your vicious pride; and after that I shall together gather you, and make you mild and meek, clean and holy, by oneing to me.*

And then I saw that each kind compassion that man hath on his even-Christians with charity, it is Christ in him.

That same noughting that was shewed in His Passion, it was shewed again here in this Compassion. Wherein were two manner of understandings in our Lord's meaning. The one was the bliss that we are brought to, wherein He willeth that we rejoice. The other is for comfort in our pain: for He willeth that we perceive that it shall all be turned to worship and profit by virtue of His passion, that we perceive that we suffer not alone but with Him, and see Him to be our Ground, and that we see His pains and His noughting passeth so far all that we may suffer, that it may not be fully thought.

The beholding of this will save us from murmuring and despair in the feeling of our pains. And if we see soothly that our sin deserveth it, yet His love excuseth us, and of His great courtesy He doeth away all our blame, and beholdeth us with ruth and pity as children innocent and unloathful.

But in this I stood beholding things general, troublously and mourning, saying thus to our Lord in my meaning, with full great dread: *Ah! good Lord, how might all be well, for the great hurt that is come, by sin, to the creature?* And here I desired, as far as I durst, to have some more open declaring wherewith I might be eased in this matter.

And to this our blessed Lord answered full meekly and with full lovely cheer, and shewed that Adam's sin was the most harm that ever was done, or ever shall be, to the world's end; and also He shewed that this [sin] is openly known in all Holy Church on earth. Furthermore He taught that I should behold the glorious Satisfaction: for this Amends-making is more pleasing to God and more worshipful, without comparison, than ever was the sin of Adam harmful. Then signifieth our blessed Lord thus in this teaching, that we should take heed to this: *For since I have made well the most harm, then it is my will that thou know thereby that I shall make well all that is less.*

FORGIVENESS OF SINS

This is a sovereign friendship of our courteous Lord that He keepeth us so tenderly while we be in sin; and furthermore He toucheth us full privily and sheweth us our sin by the sweet light of mercy and grace. But when we see our self so foul, then ween we that God were wroth with us for our sin, and then are we stirred of the Holy Ghost by contrition unto prayer and desire for the amending of our life with all our mights, to slacken the wrath of God, unto the time we find a rest in soul and a softness in conscience. Then hope we that God hath forgiven us our sins: and it is truth. And then sheweth our courteous Lord Himself to the soul—well-merrily and with glad cheer—with friendly welcoming as if it had been in pain and in prison, saying sweetly thus: *My darling I am glad thou art come to me: in all thy woe I have ever been with thee; and now seest thou my loving and we be oned in bliss.* Thus are sins forgiven by mercy and grace, and our soul is worshipfully received in joy like as it shall be when it cometh to Heaven, as oftentimes as it cometh by the gracious working of the Holy Ghost and the virtue of Christ's Passion.

Here understand I in truth that all manner of things are made ready for us by the great goodness of God, so far forth that what time we be ourselves in peace and charity, we be verily saved. But because we may not have this in fulness while we are here, therefore it falleth to us evermore to live in sweet prayer

and lovely longing with our Lord Jesus. For
He longeth ever to bring us to the fulness of
joy; as it is aforesaid, where He sheweth the
Spiritual Thirst.

But now if any man or woman because of
all this spiritual comfort that is aforesaid, be
stirred by folly to say or to think: *If this be
true, then were it good to sin [so as] to have
the more meed,*—or else to charge the less
[guilt] to sin,—beware of this stirring: for verily if it come it is untrue, and of the enemy
of the same true love that teacheth us that we
should hate sin only for love. I am sure by
mine own feeling, the more that any kind soul
seeth this in the courteous love of our Lord
God, the lother he is to sin and the more he
is ashamed. For if afore us were laid [together]
all the pains in Hell and in Purgatory and in
Earth—death and other—, and [by itself] sin,
we should rather choose all that pain than sin.
For sin is so vile and so greatly to be hated
that it may be likened to no pain which is not
sin. And to me was shewed no harder hell

than sin. For a kind soul hath no hell but sin.

And [when] we give our intent to love and meekness, by the working of mercy and grace we are made all fair and clean. As mighty and as wise as God is to save men, so willing He is. For Christ Himself is [the] ground of all the laws of Christian men, and He taught us to do good against ill: here may we see that He is Himself this charity, and doeth to us as He teacheth us to do. For He willeth that we be like Him in wholeness of endless love to ourself and to our even-Christians: no more than His love is broken to us for our sin, no more willeth He that our love be broken to ourself and to our even-Christians: but [that we] endlessly hate the sin and endlessly love the soul, as God loveth it. Then shall we hate sin like as God hateth it, and love the soul as God loveth it. And this word that He said is an endless comfort: *I keep thee securely.*

THE PATH OF PRAYER

After this our Lord shewed concerning Prayer. In which Shewing I see two conditions in our Lord's signifying: one is rightfulness, another is sure trust.

But yet oftentimes our trust is not full: for we are not sure that God heareth us, as we think because of our unworthiness, and because we feel right nought, (for we are as barren and dry oftentimes after our prayers as we were afore); and this, in our feeling our folly, is cause of our weakness. For thus have I felt in myself.

And all this brought our Lord suddenly to my mind, and shewed these words, and said: *I am Ground of thy beseeching: first it is my will that thou have it; and after, I make thee to will it; and after, I make thee to beseech it and thou beseechest it. How should it then be that thou shouldst not have thy beseeching?*

And thus in the first reason, with the three that follow, our good Lord sheweth a mighty comfort, as it may be seen in the same words. And in the first reason,—where He saith: *And thou beseechest it*, there He sheweth [His] full great pleasance, and endless meed that He will give us for our beseeching. And in the second reason, where He saith: *How should it then be?* etc., this was said for an impossible [thing]. For it is most impossible that we should beseech mercy and grace, and not have it. For everything that our good Lord maketh us to beseech, Himself hath ordained it to us from without beginning. Here may we see that our beseeching is not cause of God's goodness; and that shewed He soothfastly in all these sweet words when He saith: *I am [the] Ground.*—And our good Lord willeth that this be known of His lovers in earth; and the more that we know [it] the more should we beseech, if it be wisely taken; and so is our Lord's meaning.

Beseeching is a true, gracious, lasting will of the soul, oned and fastened into the will of our Lord by the sweet inward work of the

Holy Ghost. Our Lord Himself, He is the first receiver of our prayer, as to my sight, and taketh it full thankfully and highly enjoying; and He sendeth it up above and setteth it in the Treasure, where it shall never perish. It is there afore God with all His Holy continually received, ever spending [the help of] our needs; and when we shall receive our bliss it shall be given us for a degree of joy, with endless worshipful thanking from Him.

Full glad and merry is our Lord of our prayer; and He looketh thereafter and He willeth to have it because with His grace He maketh us like to Himself in condition as we are in kind: and so is His blissful will. Therefore He saith thus: *Pray inwardly, though thee thinketh it savour thee not: for it is profitable, though thou feel not, though thou see nought; yea, though thou think thou canst not. For in dryness and in barrenness, in sickness and in feebleness, then is thy prayer wellpleasant to me, though thee thinketh it savour thee nought but little. And so is all thy believ-*

ing prayer in my sight. For the meed and the endless thanks that He will give us, therefore He is covetous to have us pray continually in His sight. God accepteth the goodwill and the travail of His servant, howsoever we feel: wherefore it pleaseth Him that we work both in our prayers and in good living, by His help and His grace, reasonably with discretion keeping our powers [turned] to Him, till when that we have Him that we seek, in fulness of joy: that is, Jesus. And that shewed He in the Fifteenth [Revelation], farther on, in this word: *Thou shalt have me to thy meed.*

And also to prayer belongeth thanking. Thanking is a true inward knowing, with great reverence and lovely dread turning ourselves with all our mights unto the working that our good Lord stirreth us to, enjoying and thanking inwardly. And sometimes, for plenteousness it breaketh out with voice, and saith: *Good Lord, I thank Thee! Blessed mayst Thou be!* And sometime when the heart is dry and feeleth not, or else by temptation of our enemy,—then it is driven by reason and by grace to cry upon our Lord with voice, rehearsing His blessed Passion and His great Goodness; and the virtue of our Lord's word turneth into the soul and quickeneth the heart and entereth it by His grace into true working, and maketh it pray right blissfully. And truly to enjoy our Lord, it is a full blissful thanking in His sight.

Our Lord God willeth that we have true understanding, and specially in three things that belong to our prayer. The first is: *by whom and how that our prayer springeth. By whom*, He sheweth when He saith: *I am [the] Ground*; and *how*, by His Goodness: for He saith first: *It is my will*. The second is: *in what manner and how we should use our prayer*; and that is that our will be turned unto the will of our Lord, enjoying: and so meaneth He when He saith: *I make thee to will it*. The third is that we should know *the fruit and the end of our prayers*: that is, that we be oned and like to our Lord in all things;

and to this intent and for this end was all this lovely lesson shewed. And He will help us, and we shall make it so as He saith Himself;— Blessed may He be!

END TO PAIN

Afore this time I had great longing and desire of God's gift to be delivered of this world and of this life. For oftentimes I beheld the woe that is here, and the weal and the bliss that is being there: (and if there had been no pain in this life but the absence of our Lord, me-thought it was some-time more than I might bear;) and this made me to mourn, and eagerly to long. And also from mine own wretchedness, sloth, and weakness, me liked not to live and to travail, as me fell to do.

And to all this our courteous Lord answered for comfort and patience, and said these words: *Suddenly thou shalt be taken from all thy pain, from all thy sickness, from all thy distress and from all they woe. And thou shalt come up above and thou shalt have me to thy meed, and thou shalt be fulfilled of love and of bliss. And thou shalt never have no manner of pain, no manner of misliking, no wanting of will; but ever joy and bliss without end. What should it then aggrieve thee to suffer awhile, seeing that it is my will and my worship?*

And in this word: *Suddenly thou shalt be taken,*—I saw that God rewardeth man for the patience that he hath in abiding God's will, and for his time, and [for] that man lengtheneth his patience over the time of his living. For not-knowing of his time of passing, that is a great profit: for if a man knew his time, he should not have patience over that time; but, as God willeth, while the soul is in the body it seemeth to itself that it is ever at the point to be taken. For all this life and this languor that we have here is but a point, and when we are taken suddenly out of pain into bliss then pain shall be nought.

And in this time I saw a body lying on the

earth, which body shewed heavy and horrible, without shape and form, as it were a swollen quag of stinking mire. And suddenly out of this body sprang a full fair creature, a little Child, fully shapen and formed, nimble and lively, whiter than lily; which swiftly glided up into heaven. And the swollenness of the body betokeneth great wretchedness of our deadly flesh, and the littleness of the Child betokeneth the cleanness of purity in the soul. And methought: *With this body abideth no fairness of this Child, and on this Child dwelleth no foulness of this body.*

It is more blissful that man be taken from pain, than that pain be taken from man; for if pain be taken from us it may come again: therefore it is a sovereign comfort and blissful beholding in a loving soul that we shall be taken from pain. For in this behest I saw a marvellous compassion that our Lord hath in us for our woe, and a courteous promising of clear deliverance. For He willeth that we be comforted in the overpassing; and *that* He shewed in these words: *And thou shalt come up above, and thou shalt have me to thy meed, and thou shalt be fulfilled of joy and bliss.*

It is God's will that we set the point of our thought in this blissful beholding as often as we may,—and as long time keep us therein with His grace; for this is a blessed contemplation to the soul that is led of God, and full greatly to His worship, for the time that it lasteth. And [when] we fall again to our heaviness, and spiritual blindness, and feeling of pains spiritual and bodily, by our frailty, it is God's will that we know that He hath not forgotten us. And so signifieth He in these words: *And thou shalt never more have pain; no manner of sickness, no manner of misliking, no wanting of will; but ever joy and bliss without end. What should it then aggrieve thee to suffer awhile, seeing it is my will and my worship?*

It is God's will that we take His behests and His comfortings as largely and as mightily as we may take them, and also He willeth that we take our abiding and our troubles as lightly as we may take them, and set them at nought. For the more lightly we take them, and the less price we set on them, for love, the less pain we shall have in the feeling of them, and the more thanks and meed we shall have for them.

THE UNDEFEATED

This was a delectable Sight and a restful Shewing, that it is so *without end*. The beholding of this while we are here is full pleasing to God and full great profit to us; and the soul that thus beholdeth, it maketh it like to Him that is beheld, and oneth it in rest and peace by His grace. And this was a singular joy and bliss to me that I saw Him *sitting*: for the [quiet] secureness of sitting sheweth endless dwelling.

And He gave me to know soothfastly that it was He that shewed me all afore. And when I had beheld this with heedfulness, then shewed our good Lord words full meekly without voice and without opening of lips, right as He had [afore] done, and said full sweetly: *Wit it now well that it was no raving that thou sawest to-day: but take it and believe it, and keep thee therein, and comfort thee therewith, and trust thou thereto: and thou shalt not be overcome.*

These Last Words were said for believing and true sureness that it is our Lord Jesus that shewed me all. And right as in the first word that our good Lord shewed, signifying His blissful Passion,—*Herewith is the devil overcome,*—right so He said in the last word, with full true secureness, meaning us all: *Thou shalt not be overcome.* And all this teaching in this true comfort, it is general, to all mine even-Christians, as it is aforesaid: and so is God's will.

And this word: *Thou shalt not be overcome,* was said full clearly and full mightily, for assuredness and comfort against all tribulations that may come. He said not: *Thou*

*shalt not be tempested, thou shalt not be tra-
vailed, thou shalt not be afflicted*; but He said:
Thou shalt not be overcome. God willeth that
we take heed to these words, and that we be
ever strong in sure trust, in weal and woe.
For He loveth and enjoyeth us, and so willeth
He that we love and enjoy Him and mightily
trust in Him; and *all shall be well.*

And soon after, all was close and I saw no
more.

THE LORD OUR KEEPER

Our good Lord shewed the enmity of the
Fiend: in which Shewing I understood that all
that is contrary to love and peace is of his
part. And we have, of our feebleness and our
folly, to fall; and we have, of mercy and grace
of the Holy Ghost, to rise to more joy. And
if our enemy aught winneth of us by our
falling, (for it is his pleasure,) he loseth manifold more in our rising by charity and meekness. And this glorious rising, it is to him so

great sorrow and pain for the hate that he hath to our soul, that he burneth continually in envy. And all this sorrow that he would make us to have, it shall turn to himself. And for this it was that our Lord scorned him, and [it was] this [that] made me mightily to laugh.

Then is this the remedy, that we be aware of our wretchedness and flee to our Lord: for ever the more needy that we be, the more speedful it is to us to draw nigh to Him. And let us say thus in our thinking: I *know well I have a shrewd pain; but our Lord is All-Mighty and may punish me mightily; and He is All-Wisdom and can punish me discerningly; and He is All-Goodness and loveth me full tenderly.* And in this beholding it is necessary for us to abide; for it is a lovely meekness of a sinful soul, wrought by mercy and grace of the Holy Ghost, when we willingly and gladly take the scourge and chastening of our Lord that Himself will give us. And it shall be full tender and full easy, if that we will only hold us satisfied with Him and with all His works.

For the penance that man taketh of himself was not shewed me: that is to say, it was not shewed specified. But specially and highly and with full lovely manner of look was it shewed that we shall meekly bear and suffer the penance that God Himself giveth us, with mind in His blessed Passion. (For when we have mind in His blessed Passion, with pity and love, then we suffer with Him like as His friends did that saw it. And this was shewed in the Thirteenth Shewing, near the beginning, where it speaketh of Pity.) For He saith: *Accuse not [thy]self overdone much, deeming that thy tribulation and thy woe is all for thy fault; for I will not that thou be heavy or sorrowful indiscreetly. For I tell thee, howsoever thou do, thou shalt have woe. And therefore I will that thou wisely know thy penance; and [thou] shalt see in truth that all thy living is penance profitable.*

This place is prison and this life is penance, and in the remedy He willeth that we rejoice. The remedy is that our Lord is with us, keeping and leading into the fulness of joy. For this is an endless joy to us in our Lord's signifying, that He that shall be our bliss when we are there, He is our keeper while we are here. Our way and our heaven is true love and sure trust; and of this He gave understanding in all [the Shewings] and especially in the Shewing of the Passion where He made me mightily to choose Him for my heaven.

Flee we to our Lord and we shall be comforted, touch we Him and we shall be made clean, cleave we to Him and we shall be sure, and safe from all manner of peril.

For our courteous Lord willeth that we should be as homely with Him as heart may think or soul may desire. But [let us] beware that we take not so recklessly this homeliness as to leave courtesy. For our Lord Himself is sovereign homeliness, and as homely as He is, so courteous He is: for He is very courteous. And the blessed creatures that shall be in heaven with Him without end, He will have them like to Himself in all things. And to be like our Lord perfectly, it is our very salvation and our full bliss.

And if we wot not how we shall do all this, desire we of our Lord and He shall teach us: for it is His own good-pleasure and His worship; blessed may He be!

THE LESSON OF LOVE

And at the end of woe, suddenly our eyes shall be opened, and in clearness of light our sight shall be full: which light is God, our Maker and Holy Ghost, in Christ Jesus our Saviour.

Thus I saw and understood that our faith is our light in our night: which light is God, our endless Day.

The light is Charity, and the measuring of this light is done to us profitably by the wisdom of God. For neither is the light so large that we may see our blissful Day, nor is it shut from us; but it is such a light in which we may live meedfully, with travail deserving the endless worship of God. And this was seen in the Sixth Shewing where He said: *I thank thee of thy service and of thy travail.* Thus Charity keepeth us in Faith and Hope, and Hope leadeth us in Charity. And in the end all shall be Charity.

I had three manners of understanding of this light, Charity. The first is Charity unmade; the second is Charity made; the third is Charity given. Charity unmade is God; Charity made is our soul in God; Charity given is virtue. And that is a precious gift of working in which we love God, for Himself; and ourselves, in God; and that which God loveth, for God.

And in this sight I marvelled highly. For notwithstanding our simple living and our blindness here, yet endlessly our courteous Lord beholdeth us in this working, rejoicing; and of all things, we may please Him best wisely and truly to believe, and to enjoy with Him and in Him. For as verily as we shall be in the bliss of God without end, Him praising and thanking, so verily we have been in the foresight of God, loved and known in His endless purpose from without beginning. In which unbegun love He made us; and in the same love He keepeth us and never suffereth us to be hurt [in manner] by which our bliss might be lost. And therefore when the Doom is given and we be all brought up above, then shall we clearly see in God the secret things which be now hid to us. Then shall none of us be stirred to say in any wise: *Lord, if it had been thus, then it had been full well;* but we shall say all with one voice: *Lord, blessed mayst thou be, for it is thus: it is well; and now see we verily that all-thing is done as it was then ordained before that anything was made.*

This book is begun by God's gift and His grace, but it is not yet performed, as to my sight.

For Charity pray we all; [together] with *God's* working, thanking, trusting, enjoying. For thus will our good Lord be prayed to, as by the understanding that I took of all His own meaning and of the sweet words where He saith full merrily: *I am the Ground of thy beseeching.* For truly I saw and understood in our Lord's meaning that He shewed it for that He willeth to have it known more than it is: in which knowing He will give us grace to love Him and cleave to Him. For He beholdeth His heavenly treasure with so great love on earth that He willeth to give us more light and solace in heavenly joy, in drawing to Him of our hearts, for sorrow and darkness which we are in.

And from that time that it was shewed I desired oftentimes to learn what was our Lord's meaning. And fifteen years after, and more, I was answered in ghostly understanding, saying thus: *Wouldst thou learn thy Lord's meaning in this thing? Learn it well: Love was His meaning. Who shewed it thee? Love. What shewed He thee? Love. Wherefore shewed it He? For Love. Hold thee therein and thou shalt learn and know more in the same. But thou shalt never know nor learn therein other thing without end.* Thus was I learned that Love was our Lord's meaning.

And I saw full surely that ere God made us He loved us; which love was never slacked, nor ever shall be. And in this love He hath done all His works; and in this love He hath made all things profitable to us; and in this love our life is everlasting. In our making we had beginning; but the love wherein He made us was in Him from without beginning: in which love we have our beginning. And all this shall we see in God, without end.